Richard Johnson

Letters between Master Tommy and Miss Nancy Goodwill

Containing the history of their holiday amusements

Richard Johnson

Letters between Master Tommy and Miss Nancy Goodwill
Containing the history of their holiday amusements

ISBN/EAN: 9783337203559

Printed in Europe, USA, Canada, Australia, Japan

Cover: Foto ©ninafisch / pixelio.de

More available books at **www.hansebooks.com**

BETWEEN

MASTER TOMMY

AND

Miss NANCY GOODWILL;

CONTAINING THE

HISTORY

OF THEIR

HOLIDAY AMUSEMENTS.

Embellished with CUTS.

LONDON:
Printed for T. CARNAN in St. Paul's Church Yard.
MDCCLXXXVI.
[Price Six-Pence]

M A Saunders

ADVERTISEMENT.

THE very favourable Manner in which this little Work has been received, has induced the Editor of it carefully to revise the Whole, to alter many Paſſages, and expunge ſuch Parts of it as did not appear altogether properly adapted to the Improvement and Entertainment of little Maſters and Miſſes. The epiſtolary Style here adopted, is that which little Maſters and Miſſes ſhould uſe in their Correſpondence with each other, help to regulate their Judgments, to give them an early Taſte for true Politeneſs, and to inſpire them with the Love of Virtue.

MEMOIRS

OF

Master Tommy and Miss Nancy Goodwill.

MASTER *Tommy* and Miss *Nancy*, the little Authors of this pretty little Volume of Letters, are the only Children of a worthy Counsellor, who, finding his Time wholly taken up at the Bar, committed the Care of their infant Education to Mrs. Goodwill. Their Mama made it the whole Study of her Life to promote their Welfare, and form their Minds in the Manner she thought would best answer the Purpose of making them both good and happy; for it was her constant Maxim that Goodness and Happiness dwelt in the same Bosom, and were generally found to live so much together, that they could not possibly be separated.

She made it one of her chief Cares to cultivate and preserve the most perfect Love and Harmony between her Son and Daughter. During the first five or six Years they had often childish Quarrels; but their Mother always took Care to convince them of their Error in wrangling and fighting about Trifles, and to teach them how much more Pleasure they enjoyed whilst they agreed. She shewed no Partiality to either, but endeavoured to make them equal in all Things, any otherwise than that *Nancy* was taught to owe a Respect to *Tommy*, who was the Elder.

Set Hours were appointed them, in which they were regularly taught whatever was thought necessary for their Improvement, their Mamma herself daily watching the Opening of their Minds, and taking great Care to instruct them in what Manner to make the best Use of the Knowledge they attained. Whatever they read, she explained to them, and made them understand, that they might be the better for their Lessons.

When they became capable of thinking, they made it so much a Rule to obey their Parents, the

the Moment they signified their Pleasure, that by that Means they avoided many Accidents and Misfortunes. For Example: *Tommy* was one Day running giddily round the Brink of a Well, and, if he had made the least false Step, he must have fallen to the Bottom, and been drowned; but his Mamma, by a Sign with her Finger that called him to her, preserved him from the imminent Danger he was in of losing his Life; and then she took Care that they should both be the better for this little Incident, by telling them, how much their Safety and Happiness, as well as their Duty, were concerned in being obedient.

Our little Authors had once a Quarrel about something of a very trifling Nature: for such is generally the Subject of Childrens Quarrels. Though they both heartily wished to be reconciled to each other, yet did their little Hearts swell so much with Stubbornness and Pride, that neither of them would speak first. By this Means they were both uneasy, and yet would not use the Remedy that was in their own Power to remove that Uneasiness. Their Mamma found it out, and sent for Miss into the Closet, and told her, she was sorry to

see

4 MEMOIRS *of*

see her Instructions had no better Effect on her, adding, that she was ashamed of her Folly, as well as Wickedness, in thus contending with her Brother. Tears started from her Eyes which she fixed on the Ground, being too much overwhelmed with Confusion to dare to lift them up on her Mamma. On which she kindly said, that she hoped her Confusion was a sign of her Amendment; that she might indeed have made Use of her Authority, and have commanded her to seek her Brother, but she was willing, for her Good, first to convince her of her Folly. As soon as Miss *Nancy*'s Confusion would give her Leave to

speak

speak, on her Knees she gave her Mamma a thousand Thanks for her Goodness, and went immediately to seek her Brother, who joyfully embraced the first Opportunity of being reconciled to her. This Quarrel happened when Miss *Nancy* was about seven Years of Age, and Master *Tommy* about eight.

One Time, when *Tommy* and his Sister were playing in the Fields, there was a small Rivulet stopped *Nancy* in her Way. *Tommy* being nimble, and better able to jump than his Sister, with one Spring leaped over, and left his Sister behind; but seeing her uneasy that she could not get over to him, his Good-nature prompted him to go back and assist her. On this their Mamma bid *Nancy* remember, how much her Brother's superior strength might assist her in his being her Protector, and that she ought in return to use her utmost Endeavours to oblige him; by which means they would be mutual Assistants to each other throughout Life. Thus every Thing that passed, this wise Parent made Use of to improve their Understandings, and amend their Hearts.

They

They were very early inſtructed to beware of all Kinds of Deceit; ſo that they were accuſtomed to confeſs a Fault, rather than tell a Falſity to conceal it. Though the Friendſhip between them was ſo ſtrongly cultivated, yet they were taught, that telling Lies for each other, or praiſing each other when it was not deſerved, was not only a Fault, but a very great Crime, and encouraging one another in Wickedneſs and Folly.

When *Nancy* was about eight Years old, ſhe had a Cat that ſhe had bred up from a little Kitten, which uſed to play around her, till ſhe had indulged for the poor Animal a Fondneſs, that made her delight to have it continually with her wherever ſhe went; and, in Return for her Indulgence, the Cat ſeemed to have changed its Nature, and aſſumed the Manner which more properly belongs to Dogs; for it would follow her about the Houſe and Garden, mourn at her Abſence, and rejoice at her Preſence.

Miſs *Nancy* was at laſt ſo accuſtomed to ſee this little Friſk (for ſo ſhe called it) playing round her, that ſhe ſeemed to miſs Part of herſelf

self in its Absence. One Day the poor little Creature followed *Nancy* to the Door, when a Parcel of School-Boys coming by, one of them catched her up in his Arms, and ran away with her. All her Cries were to no Purpose; for he was out of Sight with her in a Moment, and there was no Method to trace his Steps. The cruel Boys, for Sport, as they called it, hunted it the next Day from one to the other, in the most barbarous Manner, till at last it took Shelter in that House which used to be its Protection, where it expired at *Nancy's* Feet.

She was so struck with the Sight of poor Puss dying in that Manner, that the great Grief of her Heart overflowed at her Eyes, and she was for some Time inconsolable.

Her indulging Mamma comforted without blaming her, till she thought she had had sufficient Time to vent her Grief, and then sending for her into her Chamber, thus admonished her:

" *Nancy*, I have watched you ever since the Death of your favourite Cat, and have been
in

in Hopes daily, that your Lamentations and Melancholy on that Account would be at an End! but I still find you grieving, as if such a Loss was irreparable. Now, though I have always encouraged you in all Sentiments of Good-nature and Compassion, and am sensible, that where these Sentiments are strongly implanted, they will extend their Influence even to the least Animal; yet you are to consider, my Child, that you are not to give Way to any Passions that interfere with your Duty: For whenever there is any Contention between your Duty and your Inclinations, you must conquer the latter, or become wicked and contemptible. If, therefore, you give Way to this Melancholy, how will you be able to perform your Duty towards me, in cheartfully obeying my Commands, and endeavouring by your lively Prattle and innocent Gaiety of Heart, to be my Companion and Delight: Nor will you be fit to converse with your Brother, whom I have endeavoured to educate in such a Manner, that I hope he will be a Parent to you, if you deserve his Love and Protection. In short, if you do not keep Command enough of yourself to prevent being ruffled by every Accident, you will be
unfit

unfit for all the social Affairs of Life, and be despised by all those, whose Regard and Love are worth your seeking. I treat you, my Girl, as one capable of considering what is for your own Good; for, though you are but eight Years of Age, yet I hope the Pains I have taken in explaining all you read, and in answering all your Questions in Search of Knowledge, have not been so much thrown away, but that you are more capable of judging, than those unhappy Children are, whose Parents have neglected to instruct them. And, therefore, farther to enforce what I say, remember, that repining at any Accident that happens to you, is an Offence to the Almighty, to whom I have taught you daily to pray, and to return Thanks for his Blessings. I expect therefore, *Nancy*, that you now dry up your Tears, and resume your usual Chearfulness in my Sight. But you will deceive yourself, if you think that alone is performing your Duty: If you would obey me as you ought, you must try heartily to root from your Mind all Sorrow and Gloominess. You may depend upon it, this Command is in your Power to obey; for, you know, I never require any Thing of you that is impossible."

After her Mamma had thus spoken, she went out to take a Walk in the Garden, and left *Nancy* to consider of what she had said. The Moment she came to reflect seriously, she found it was indeed in her Power to root all Melancholy from her Heart, when she considered it was necessary, in order to perform her Duty to God, to obey the best of Mothers, and to make herself a Blessing and a chearful Companion to her rather than a Burthen, and the Cause of her Uneasiness, by her foolish Melancholy.

This little Accident, as managed by her Mamma, has been a Lesson to Master *Tommy* and Miss *Nancy* in governing their Passions ever since. It would be endless to repeat all the Methods this good Mother invented for their Instruction, Amendment and Improvement. Suffice it to say, that she contrived every Day to open some new Scene of Knowledge.

Master *Tommy*, on his Side, did every Thing that lay in his Power to amuse his Sister. He would sometimes cut Maps to Pieces, in such a Manner, as to separate one County from another, and then, mixing them together, would
set

Master Tommy and Miss Nancy.   11

fet his Sister to replace them: By this Means he made her a tolerable good Geographer, at an Age long before Children in general begin to think of any such Thing. At another Time, they would learn some moral Dialogue by Heart, and then speak it before their Mamma, with all the Propriety of Action and Utterance they were capable of.

Mr. and Mrs. Goodwill would frequently laugh heartily, on seeing their two little ones, on a Summer's Moon light Night, setting Side by Side on the Grass-Plat before the

House, and peeping through a Telescope to discover the Mountains in th Moon. Indeed,

B 2

they

they accustomed themselves so much to this Kind of Diversion, that they had given Names to many of the brightest Stars in the Heavens, the most remarkable of which were called after their most favourite Play-fellows, and those of less Magnitude, after those they less esteemed.

In this Manner they lived till Master *Tommy* was twelve, and Miss *Nancy* eleven Years of Age, when their Parents thought it most adviseable to give them a superior Education to what they were likely to gain at Home. They were therefore sent to two different Boarding-Schools: But I will pass over the Grief felt on all Sides at Parting. Master *Tommy*, however, had not been long at School, before he sent his Sister *Nancy* the following Piece of Poetry, as his first Attempt of that Kind. It is an Ode to *Virtue*, which he desired his Sister would stick up in the Arbour, where she and her little School-fellows assembled every Evening.

Virtue, soft Balm of every Woe,
 Of ev'ry Grief the Cure,
'Tis thou alone that canst bestow
 Pleasures unmix'd and pure.

> The shady Wood, the verdant Mead,
>   Are *Virtue's* flow'ry Road;
> Nor painful are the Steps which lead
>   To her divine Abode.
>
> 'Tis not in Palaces nor Halls,
>   She or her Train appear:
> Far off she flies from pompous Walls;
>   *Virtue* and *Peace* dwell here.

It was the Holidays following that they wrote the Letters, (which form this little Volume) to each other. How much is it to be wished, that every Parent, and every Child, would pursue the same Steps! we should not then meet with so many wretched and unhappy Parents, nor so many undutiful and wicked Children.

LETTERS

BETWEEN

r TOMMY and Miss NANCY.

Miss Nancy *to Master* Tommy.

Dear Tommy,

I AM very sory to find, that my late Illness will prevent me from seeing you these Holidays, my Governess being of Opinion, that the Length of the Journey, and the Heat of the Weather, are Obstacles I am not yet in a Condition to engage with. I had formed many Devices to amuse you, myself, and my little Companions, in-Town; but, though I am disappointed in this View, do not imagine that I shall suffer you to spend these Holidays in Idleness: I shall so trouble you with Letters, that you will find all your Time employed in writing me Answers.

Two

Two or three of my School-fellows are detained here by the same misfortune, and two or three more stay entirely out of Kindness to keep us Company. We therefore propose to form ourselves into a little Society during this Recess, and have already, my dear *Tommy*, chosen you our Governor, even though we cannot have your Company. I am chosen Secretary, and am to send you an Account of what passes among us. You, in Return, are to point out our Mistakes, to direct us in the Pursuit of Knowledge, and to furnish us with such Materials, as may answer the intended Purpose.

However

16 LETTERS *between*

However laborious such a Task may be to you, I am sure, it will not be disagreeable, when your *Nancy* requests it. You will give my most dutiful Respects to my Papa and Mamma, my kindest Wishes to all my little Companions in Town, and believe me, my dear *Tomny*,

LET.

LETTER II.

Master TOMMY *to Miss* NANCY.

Dear Nancy,

I AM at all Times very sorry to hear that you are in the least indisposed; but I am more particularly unhappy, when the Consequence of it is the Loss of your Company. It will however afford me the most pleasing Satisfaction, if I can be any Ways instrumental in amusing you. But pray, Miss, I hope you and your little Society are not going to turn Philosophers! If you are, I shall put you in Mind of your Needles, your Pins, and your Thread Papers. Leave those Subjects to us Boys (I was going to say Men) and we may perhaps, now and then, condescend to give you some short Lectures upon those Matters.

In the mean Time, I must advise you *little Folks*

Folks (for the Honour you have conferred on me makes me think myself great indeed) to take Care that you do not fall out among yourselves; for Arguments, among us Boys, are often productive of Wranglings; and pardon me, my pretty little Misses, if I should say, that yours are not wholly free from those Accidents. However, you see that I wish to be both merry and serious: when it is your Pleasure that I shall laugh, nobody shall do it more heartily; and, when it is your Pleasure I shall be serious, I will then be as grave as a Judge. Without further Preamble, I wait your future Commands, and am, with the greatest Respect to the young Ladies, my dearest *Nancy,*

Your ever affectionate Brother,

T. GOODWILL.

LETTER III.

Miss Nancy *to Master* Tommy.

Dear Tommy,

IN the first Place, I have to thank you for the tender Manner in which you express your Concern for me, and your Readiness to oblige me. In the next Place, by Virtue of the Office I bear in our little Society, I must acquaint you, that last Night a Motion was made among us. " That the unanimous Thanks of this Society be returned to Master *Tommy*, for the kind Letter he has obliged this Society with; and that he be desired to continue his Favours during the Holidays." The Question was no sooner put than carried: So that you see, you have got a fine deal of Business on your Hands!

Our Debates then turned upon what Animal was the noblest.—Do not think my dear *Tommy*, that we were going to philosophise;
no,

no, no, we debated it in a very familiar Manner. For my Part, I infifted on the Lion, Mifs *Patty* on the Squirrel, Mifs *Fanny* on the Lap Dog, and Mifs *Debby* on the winged Chorifters. In fhort, Debates ran fo high, that, as there was no Probability of fettling it among ourfelves, we agreed to beg the Favour of our Governefs to determine the Point in Queftion. You know Madam is very obliging; you will not therefore wonder at her favouring us with the following agreeable Harangue.

" *My little Pupils*,

If Cuftom had not dignified the *Lion* with the awful Title of the *King of Beafts*, Reafon would undoubtedly have beftowed it upon the *Horfe*. The Lion has certainly no Manner of Right to it—he is rather an Ufurper and a Tyrant: for he makes no other Ufe of his Prerogative, than either to devour his Subjects, or infpire them with Horror and Amazement. The Horfe, on the other Hand, neither injures his Fellow Creatures in their Perfons, nor attempts to invade their Properties: He does nothing to render himfelf the Object of Hatred or Contempt. No bad Qualities can

can juftly be afcribed to him; and, in fact, he is poffeffed of all fuch as are amiable and praife worthy. There is no Animal whatever fo complete, with refpect to its Symmetry and Proportion, has a more graceful Spirit, is more liberal in his Services, and more abftemious in his Diet,

Caft your Eyes on all other Animals, of what Kind foever, do you find one that has fo beautiful a Head, or Eyes fo fparkling or full of Fire? One whofe Neck is cloathed with equal Majefty, and whofe Mane waves in the Wind with fo much Grandeur? Whether he be under the Direction of his Rider, or at his

his own Liberty to range in the Fields without Controul, we obferve in him a noble Deportment, and an Air which ftrikes the Eye of every Beholder, though infenfible of all his own Perfections, with an agreeable Surprife.

His inclinations are ftill more engaging: He can properly be faid to have but one, and that is, to be as ferviceable as poffible to his Mafter. If it is expected he fhould drag the Plough, or carry any Burthen, how heavy foever, he is always ready and willing. If the Owner chufes to ride him, he feems confcious of the Honour, and ufes his utmoft Endeavours to pleafe him; at the leaft Signal he alters his Pace, and either walks, trots, or gallops, as required. Neither the Length of his Journey, the Badnefs of the Roads, neither Hedges nor Ditches, nor even the moft rapid Rivers, difcourage him; he flies, like a Bird, over every Obftacle that would give a Check to his Career.

Is there any further Service expected from him; Is it incumbent on him to defend his Mafter or bear him to an Engagement?—He goes on to meet the armed Foe, he mocks
Fear,

Fear, and is not afraid ; the Sound of the Trumpet and the Drum infpire him with frefh Ardour, and he turns not back even from the Sword.

Next to the Horfe, my little Pupils, I rank that ufeful Animal the *Dog*. Of all the Accomplifhments which a Dog is capable of attaining, there is not, doubtlefs, any one half fo confiderable, as that inviolable Friendfhip and undaunted Courage, which he fhews for his Mafter on all Occafions: and it is very plain that the *Deity* configned the Dog to Man, to ferve him as a faithful Companion, Affiftant and Protector: The Services we receive from Dogs are, indeed, as various as their Species.

The Maftiff and the Bull-Dog guard our Houfes in the Night, and referve all their Fury and Refentment for that Seafon, wherein neceffitous Vagrants may form their wicked Defigns againft us. The Shepherd's Dog is qualified to attack the Wolf, when he worries his Sheep, and to regulate the Flock.

Among the various Claffes of Sporting-Dogs,

Dogs, the Terrier has very fhort Legs, to enable him to bury himfelf in the Grafs, or break his Way through a Quickfet Hedge. Nature has beftowed on the Greyhound a fharp Head and flender Body, in order to cut the Air with more Eafe, and purfue his Game with greater Expedition; his long, thin Legs foon ftretch over a large Tract of Ground: he exceeds even the Hare in Point of Swiftnefs, whofe Safety, therefore, principally depends on his Doublings and Turnings, and other Arts of Flight. There are divers Kinds of thefe Animals whofe Names vary according to their refpective Qualifications; All of them, however, are equally eager for the Sport, and faithful in the due Difcharge of their feveral Offices.

In fhort, amidft all thefe various domeftic Animals, which are fo tractable, and fo unavoidly attached to their Owner's Intereft, there is not one, even down to the Spaniel and the Dane, but what renders himfelf, in fome Degree, amiable by his Sprightlinefs and Activity, valuable by his indefatigable Induftry, and fometimes ferviceable by his Diligence, and the timely Notice he gives his Mafter of

fome

some approaching Danger in the Night, when all the Family perhaps are sleeping. The Horse and the Dog, in short, are the only two Animals, on whose Friendship and Fidelity we can with Safety depend; for which Reason the old Proverb says, *A Man, a Horse, and a Dog, are never tired of each other's Company.*"

Our Governess here finished, and left us, as she apprehended she had fully satisfied us in our present Enquiry. No sooner was Madam gone, than Miss *Fanny*, who had before pleaded hard for the Nobility of her Lap-Dog, claimed the Pre-eminence of Judgment; but as we could not find out that her pretty *Cæsar* was possibly of any other Use than that of sometimes eating the spare Leg or Wing of a Fowl, which ought to be given to some poor Creature, we absolutely denied her Claim. But, my dear *Tommy*, I fear I grow tedious. Adieu for the present.

A. GOODWILL.

LETTER IV.

Master Tommy *to Miss* Nancy.

Dear Nancy,

I Cannot but smile when I reflect, that you was obliged to give up your fierce Lion to the more noble and useful Animal the Horse. It is, however, a Matter of some Consolation to you, that you are not the only one who has adopted that Opinion; but, I think, your Governess, has so clearly settled the Matter, that there certainly remains nothing for me to say on that Subject.

I should with the greatest Pleasure, my dear Nancy, have endeavoured to send you something entertaining; but a most terrible Accident has happened to me since I last wrote to you. I endeavoured to forget it, and, though I cannot accomplish that End at present, yet I hope, by the Time I receive your next Favour, I shall in some Degree have repaired the Loss,

and

and be then in a Condition to write; but let me beg of you (as I know your tender Difpofition) not even to mention it to me hereafter, as I fhould be forry to have my Grief renewed.—O my dear Nancy, how fhall I tell you that my fweet Kite, which boafted of the two fineft Glafs Eyes perhaps ever feen, which was fo crouded with Stars, and which coft me fuch immenfe Labour, is loft—loft for ever! A fudden Guft of Wind fnapped the Twine, my dear Kite fell into the River, and was carried away by the Tide. What Lofs I may have fuffered in my Twine, I am not yet able to afcertain; but I fear I fhall find it confiderable. I am unable at prefent to fay more, than that I am, dear Sifter,

Your unfortunate Brother,

T. GOODWILL.

LETTER V.

Miss Nancy *to Master* Tommy.

Dear Tommy,

I Have been ordered to send you the following little Story for your Amusement. You have imposed upon me a disagreeable Silence; but I must say no more.

Cha-Abbas, a famous King of *Persia*, being on a Tour to visit Part of his extensive Dominions, withdrew from the Multitude that surrounded him, in Order to visit the most lonely Villages, that he might there behold, without being known, Mankind in all its natural and unaffected Freedom. For this Purpose, he took with him only one of his Courtiers, who was his favourite Companion.

I am totally ignorant, said the King to his Attendant, of the true and genuine Characters of Mankind. Confined within the narrow Limits

Limits of a Court, I see but little, and even that little is disguised. I long to be accquainted with the Simplicity and Happiness of a rural Life, and to converse with those, who, though so little thought of, indeed despised, are nevertheless the real Support of all human Society. I am weary of a Life among Sycophants, who take every Opportunity to deceive me, and enrich themselves whilst they flatter me. It is necessary that I should visit Husbandmen and Shepherds, to whom I am an utter Stranger.

The King travelled with his Confidant through several Villages, where the Peasants were dancing to the Sound of the Tabor and the Pipe, He was overjoyed to see that his Subjects, though at some Distance from the Capital, had their Diversions and Amusements, and of a Kind so innocent and so inexpensive. Growing tired with their Journey, they refreshed themselves in a Cottage, and being very hungry with walking farther than usual, the homely Provision they there met with seemed more agreeable to the King, than all the studied and exquisite Dainties of his own Table.

Passing

Paſſing over a Meadow, enamelled with Flowers, which decked the Borders of a limpid Stream, he caſt his Eyes on a young Shepherd, playing in melodious Strains on his Pipe

beneath a ſhady Palm-Tree, whilſt his Flock were grazing round about him. The King approached him, ſurveyed him cloſely, and found his Aſpect agreeable, and his Air, though eaſy and natural, yet graceful and majeſtic. The Simplicity of his Dreſs no Ways diminiſhed the Luſtre of his Perſon, or the Sweetneſs of his Countenance.

The

The King at first supposed him to be some Person of an illustrious Birth, who had disguised himself for some particular Purpose; but, upon conversing with the Shepherd, he learned that his Parents lived in an adjacent Village, and that his Name was *Alibeg*. The more Questions the King put to him, the more he admired the Strength and Solidity of his Genius. His Eyes were lively, and yet had nothing in them wild or glaring; his Voice was sweet, moving and melodious; his Features were not strong, neither were they soft and effeminate.

Alibeg, though sixteen years of Age, was not conscious of those Perfections, which were so conspicuous to others. He supposed that his Thoughts, his Conversation, and his Person, were the very same as his Neighbours. Without Education, he understood every Thing that Reason dictates to those, who listen to her Admonitions,

The King, after a familiar Interview, was charmed with his Conversation; for *Alibeg* informed him of the State of the People—a Truth which Sovereigns never learn from the
Crowd

Crowd of fawning Sycophants that furround them. He frequently fmiled at the innocent Freedom of the Youth, whofe Anfwers were all void of Art and Deceit. It was an agreeable Novelty to the King, to hear him talk without the leaft Referve. He gave the Courtier, who accompanied him, a private Signal, not to difcover that he was the King; for fear *Alibeg*, if he once knew with whom he was converfing, fhould in an Inftant lofe his wonted Freedom, which would have obfcured for the prefent all his other Graces.

I am now convinced, faid the Prince to his Courtier, that Nature is as beautiful in the loweft Station, as in the higheft. No Monarch's Son was ever born with nobler Faculties than this young Shepherd. I fhould think myfelf infinitely happy had I a Son fo beautiful, fo amiable, and fo difcreet. He feems to me to have a promifing Genius; and, if he be but duly inftructed, he will doubtlefs, in Procefs of Time, become a great Man. I will have him educated in my own Court.

The King accordingly took *Alibeg* away with him, who was much furprized to find,
that

that a Prince should be so pleased with his Conversation. He was first taught to read, write and sing, and afterwards improved, by proper Tutors, in all the Arts and Sciences which adorn the Mind. At first he was somewhat startled at the Grandeur of the Court; and his sudden Revolution of Fortune, in some Measure, influenced his Temper. His Youth, and the King's Favour together, wrought too visible a Change in his Prudence and Moderation. His Crook, his Pipe, and Shepherd's Dress, were now forgotten, and instead thereof he appeared in a purple Robe, embroidered with Gold, and a Turban enriched with Jewels. He made a more agreeable Figure than any one at Court, and was qualified to transact the most important Affairs, and merited the Confidence of his Master, who, conscious of *Alibeg*'s refined Taste for Grandeur, conferred on him at last one of the most advantageous Posts in all *Persia*, which was that of Jewel-Keeper and Treasurer of his Houshold.

During the whole Reign of the great *Cha-Abbas*, *Alibeg*'s Reputation daily encreased. The more he advanced in Years, the oftener he he reflected on his former State of Life, and sometimes with Regret.—O happy Days! would he whisper to himself—O innocent Days! Days since which I have never seen one so pleasant! Shall I never see you more? He, who has deprived me of you, by making me thus great, has utterly undone me!

Alibeg determined to revisit his native Village: he gazed with Fondness on all those Places, where he had formerly danced, sung, and tuned his Pipe with his Fellow Swains. He made some Kind of Presents to all his Friends and Relations; but advised them, as they valued their Peace of Mind, never to resign their rural Pleasures, never to experience the Anxieties and Misfortunes of a Court.

Alibeg felt those Anxieties and Misfortunes himself soon after the Death of his good Master *Cha-Abbas*, who was succeeded by *Cha-Sephi*. Some envious artful Courtiers found Means to prejudice the young Prince against *Alibeg*. He has, said they, betrayed the Trust reposed in him by the late King. He has hoarded up immense Treasures to his
own

own Use, and embezzled several valuable Effects with which he was entrusted.

Cha-Sephi was young, and withal a Monarch, which was more than sufficient to make him credulous, remiss, and indiscreet: He had the Vanity to think himself qualified to reform his father's Actions, and judge of Things better than he. To have some Plea for removing *Alibeg* from his Post, he charged him, pursuant to the Advice of his malicious Courtiers, to produce the Scymetar set with Diamonds of an immense Value, which his royal Grandsire used to wear in Battle. *Cha-Abbas* had formerly ordered those costly Decorations to be taken out, and *Alibeg* brought sufficient Evidence to prove, that they were so removed, by express Command of the late King, long before his Promotion to that Office.

When *Alibeg*'s Enemies found this Scheme too weak to effect his Ruin, they prevailed on *Cha-Sephi* to give him strict Orders to produce, within a Fortnight, an exact Inventory of all the rich Furniture entrusted to his Care. No one Article was missing, every Thing was clean,

clean, in its proper Place, and preserved with the greatest Carefulness. The King, surprised to see such Order and Regularity every where observed, began to entertain a favourable Opinion of *Alibeg*, till he espied, at the End of a long Gallery, full of the richest Furniture, an Iron Door, with three strong Locks. There it is, whispered the envious Courtiers in his Ear, that *Alibeg* has concealed all the valuable Effects, which be has purloined from you. Thereupon the King in a Passion cried out, I will see what is in that Room! What have you concealed there? Shew me!

Alibeg, thereupon, fell prostrate at his Feet, conjuring him, in the Name of God, not to dispossess him of all he held valuable upon Earth. It is not just, said he, that I should lose at once all that I am worth, all my future Dependance, after having served your royal Father so many Years. Strip me, if you think fit of every Thing besides, but leave me this.

Cha-Sephi now took it for granted, that all *Alibeg*'s ill-gotten Treasure lay concealed there. He exalted his Voice, and peremptorily commanded the Door to be opened.

At

At length, *Alibeg*, who had the Key in his Pocket, unlocked it himself. Nothing, however, was found there, but his Crook, his Pipe, and the rural Habit which he wore in his Youth, and often viewed with Pleasure, for Fear he should forget his mean Extraction.—
" Behold, great Sir, said he, the valuable Re-
" mains of my former Felicity, which neither
" Fortune, nor your Majesty have taken from
" me. Behold my Treasure, which I reserve to
" make me rich, when you shall think proper
" to make me poor. Take back every Thing
" besides, but leave me these dear Pledges of
" my rural Station. These are my substantial
" Riches, which will never fail me; these are
" simple, innocent, and ever grateful to all such
" as can live contented with the Necessaries of
" Life, and never torment themselves about su-
" perfluous Enjoyments; these are Riches, which
" are possessed with Liberty and Safety; these
" are Riches, which never gave me one Mo-
" ment's Disquiet. O ye dear Implements of a
" plain but happy life! I value none but you;
" with you I will live and die? Why have these
" false alluring Riches thus deluded me, and
" robbed me of my Repose! I here resign, great
" Sir, the many favours which your royal
Bounty

"Bounty has bestowed on me. I will only re-
"serve what I had, when the King, your Fa-
"ther, by his Munificence made me miserable."

The King, upon this Declaration, was convinced of *Alibeg's* Innocence: and, resenting the Perfidiousness of those Courtiers, who conspired his Downfal, banished them from Court.

Alibeg became his Prime Minister, and was entrusted with the most important Secrets. He visited, however, every Day, his Crook, his Pipe, and rural Habit, which he always kept locked up in his Treasury, that he might have them ready whenever fickle Fortune should throw him out of Favour: He died in a good old Age, without the least Inclination to have his Enemies punished, or to encrease his Possessions, and left his Relations no more than what would decently maintain them in the Station of Shepherds, which he always thought the safest and most happy.

Here, my dear *Tommy*, closes the Story; but, I suppose, you will expect I should draw some Moral from it, and such a one as may convince you, that I do not read without reflecting.

flecting.—Well, then, in *Alibeg* we see what the Force of a natural Genius, and good Fortune, may raise a man to. In him we see likewise, that the most exalted Station is not always able to procure Ease and Satisfaction of Mind, and that we are no where surer of finding it than among Peasants and homely Villagers, where Cause for Envy seldom dwells. The base Schemes of the invidious Courtiers, who aimed at nothing less than the total Ruin of the honest and innocent *Alibeg*, which at last turned on themselves, verifies that old Saying, Though Falsity and Calumny may a while gain Ground, yet Truth and Justice shall at last prevail.

I remain,

Your affectionate Sister,

A. GOODWILL.

LET-

LETTER VI.

Master Tommy *to Miss* Nancy.

Dear Nancy,

I AM much obliged to you for your last entertaining Story; and, as the Affair of my kite is now become rather a Matter of Laughter than Sorrow, (though I must still say it was a sweet one) I shall, in my turn, endeavour to amuse you, and the rest of your amiable Society.

Mr. *Addison*, in one of the *Spectators*, has taken Notice, that there is more Ceremony observed in settling the Punctilios of a Country Visit, than in regulating the Meeting of a whole Bench of Justices: The Story I am now going to tell you is taken from real Life.

In a Village, about ten Miles from *Bath*, there lived a happy Couple, whom I shall call by their Christian Names, *John* and *Joan*.
Than

Than *John*, who was a Farmer and Grazier, no Man in the Country could better diftinguifh good from bad Corn, or knew the different Kinds of Beafts at a Country Fair, fo as to chufe the beft from the worft Sort; nor could they produce fuch excellent Grain, or breed fuch fine Cattle. His Fame was every where rung, and he was pointed out as the greateft Example for Men of his profeffion to follow. But if *John* was fkilful in his Sphere, *Joan* was not lefs fo in her's: Nay, it has been doubted by profeffed Judges, whether fhe had not the Superiority; for no Woman in the Country could churn her cream fo gracefully, and make it rife fo quick, to produce excellent Butter, or had fuch profound Judgment in making that ftaple Commodity of the Country, Cheefe. In fhort, no Couple in *Wiltfhire* were fuch Artifts in their Way of Bufinefs, as they were univerfally confeffed to be.

It is not to be wondered at, as they were unincumbered as yet with any Children, that they were in a fine Way of living, as it is termed. No Man more punctually paid his Rent than *John*. His Landlord, who was the
'Squire

'Squire of the Parish, a few Miles from the Farm our Rustic rented of him, was charmed with his Punctuality, and could not but think himself happy in such a good Tenant. Instead of raising his Rent, agreeable to the Custom of the World, when he saw he chearfully paid it, he was greatly rejoiced to find him in a thriving Condition, and often shewed him signal Marks of it.

One time, in particular, when fifty-three Pounds were due for half a Year's Rent, the 'Squire sent his Footman to desire *John* and his Wife to dine with him, and mentioned the Day. He thanked the 'Squire for this Invitation, and promised to accept of it.

John and *Joan* were now very busy in preparing for the Visit, and, till the appointed Time, could not help often giving each other some Hints, that as the 'Squire was a very well-bred Gentleman, and his Lady a Woman of great Gentility, they must not behave before them in the Manner they did at Home.

The Time being arrived, *John* put his Money into his Leather Purse, dressed himself in
the

the finest Apparel he had, saddled old *Dobbin*, and, taking his Wife behind him, who was spruced out in her finest Geer, set out.

Upon the Road *Joan* seemed mighty diffident about her Husband's Behaviour, and told him so in plain Terms; but *John* cut her off with an " Oddzooks, *Joan*, dost think I am a Fool? I warrant ye, I'll 'have myself as well as the best o'um.".

On their Arrival in the Court-Yard they alighted, and consigned old *Dobbin* to the Care of a Servant, whom *John* particularly charged to take Care of him, and he would remember him when he went away.

The Couple now entered the House, and going into the Kitchen, in order to be ushered in to the 'Squire and his Lady, they saw a Gentleman with a Bag-Wig and Ruffles, whom they supposed to be the 'Squire's Brother, or some Relation; they bowed and curtsyed to him for some Time, telling him, they were his Honour's Servants: But he assuring them he was only my Lady's Footman, on being acquainted with their Business, shewed them into the parlour, where his Master and Mistress were sitting.

The Gentleman was reading the News-paper to his Lady, but on his Tenant's Approach he ceased, and rose up to receive his Guests, who were so long scraping and curtsying, that it was imagined they never would cease. The 'Squire and his Lady received the Visitors with that easy Freedom, which distinguishes People that have seen the World; and, desiring them to be seated, after no little scraping and curtsying, they obeyed.

The 'Squire and *John* now entered into Discourse on Farming and Grazing, and the latter gave such pertinent Answers, and made such

such shrewd Remarks, as plainly shewed he was Master of the Subject. In the mean Time the Lady and *Joan* were conversing on the Management of the Dairy.

Hitherto every Thing had gone on well; but the 'Squire letting the News-paper fall out of his Hand, and stooping for it, received a great Blow on the Head, which almost stunned him. How this Affair happened, it will be necessary to explain. *John*, whose Eyes were fixed on the Paper, even before it had reached the Ground, not being willing to be thought deficient in Point of Good-Manners, started from his Chair, and ran to take it up. *Joan* casually seeing her Husband rise and viewing the Occasion of it, was resolved he should not have the Honour of restoring it to the 'Squire; and flying, swift as thought, to execute her Intent, she had no sooner her Hand on the unlucky Paper, than her Head meeting *John*'s received a violent Percussion. Her Head being as thin as *John*'s was thick, could not resist the mighty Blow, but sunk under it; and, before it had reached the Ground, meeting the 'Squire's occasioned the Misfortune before-mentioned. As to *John* he he having a Leaden Head, could not scarce feel it; but his Wife's poor Paper Skull was almost cracked. The 'Squire and his Lady, seeing her prostrate on the Floor, both endeavoured to lift her up, which they effected, without meeting the like Misfortune of the unfortunate Couple.

John, in the mean Time, was standing in Amaze, and scratching his Head with all his Fingers; but, seeing his Wife's Condition, he took her by the Hand, and asked her what was the Matter with her? The poor Woman could not reply; but a Glass of Wine being administered to her, after some Time, she again recovered.

After this Affair, *John* looked very silly for some Time; but the Dinner being now ready, he was determined to redeem his Honour, by imitating the 'Squire in every Thing, and then he knew he could not err.

John and *Joan*, after no few Curtseys, took their Seats; though *John* could not be reconciled to the thoughts of sitting above the 'Squire, notwithstanding he was told, that
the

the Master of the Family always sat at the lowest Place, and for some Time *John* would not give up the Point; but the Lady helping him to a Slice of Roast Beef, he was forced to consent.

Though the 'Squire had gained this Victory, yet he must not expect *John* will obey him in every Thing; for in Spite of all his Entreaties, he would not come within a Yard of the Table, but kept at a proper Distance. Flourishing his Knife and Fork, and whetting them on each other, in Imitation of a Butcher, and next rubbing the former on his nice Buckskin Breeches, he cut away and acted like a man that was no Novice in the Business. The Gentleman now called for some Ale, *John* did the same, drank his Service to his Wife, and his Love to the Lady.

As *John* had resolved to mimic the 'Squire's so *Joan* had determined to copy the Lady's Behaviour. In Consequence of this, whenever the Lady called for Bread, *Joan* called; when the Lady called for Ale or Wine, *Joan* did so likewise.

John, who was now almoſt ſatisfied, was reſolved to imitate his Landlord, in calling for a Glaſs of Wine; and it being brought, he imagined he ſhould pay him and his Lady greater Reſpect in drinking it ſtanding. He therefore roſe up, and performed with no little Grace.

Joan, now thinking herſelf eclipſed by *John*'s ſuperior Brightneſs, thought ſhe muſt do the like, and receiving it, agreeable to her Call, ſhe ſtood up and drank her Love to the 'Squire. Looking over her Shoulder on the Footman, and ſeeing him laugh, ſhe gave her Service to him; but as ill Fate would have it, in reinſtating her Head in its former Poſition, ſhe hit ſo violently againſt the Glaſs as ſplit every Drop of it on the Lady's Cap, Handkerchief, and Gown, who unfortunately ſat next her. She was now confuſed and under a greater Eclipſe than before; but the Lady telling her no Harm was done, ſhe received another Glaſs of Wine, and performed the Ceremony with as much Elegance as *John* had.

There happened to be ſome Peaſe Soup on the

the Table, which *John* did not chuse to eat before his Meat; but declared it was the best Way to eat it after, in order, as he said, to fill up the Chinks. The Lady now helping him to a large plateful, the 'Squire was going to hand it to him: But *John* knew good Manners better; and taking it out of the Gentlewoman's Hands, to save him the Trouble, he did it so hastily, that he overturned it on a Plate of Apple-Pye, the 'Squire had just helped himself to.

This was a sad Stroke upon poor *John*; but he had scarcely resolved how to excuse himself, ere *Joan* apologized to the Lady for her Husband's Ignorance. Misfortunes seldom come alone! for when she was in the Middle of her Apology, a Bit happened to go the wrong Way, which set her coughing the Apple-Pye full in the Lady's Face. The Couple were now both confounded, and knew not how to frame any further Apology; but the Lady applying her Handkerchief to her Face, and the 'Squire talking on some other Subject, relieved the poor Creatures from the unhappy Dilemma into which they were reduced.

At length, however, Dinner was over. *John* and *Joan* had paid the best Compliment they could to the Entertainment, for between them they had eaten seven or eight Pounds.

Now they withdrew into another Room, and, after the Bottles and Glasses were set in due Form, *John* produced his Leather Purse in order to pay the 'Squire; but, unfortunately, *John* had miscounted the Money, and was deficient in Half a Guinea; and, as he had only Seventeen Pence in his Pocket besides, which he knew would be insufficient, he asked *Joan*, whether she could make up the Sum. *Joan* immediately produced her Snuff-Box, and took out of it nine Shillings and Sixpence, which she paid the 'Squire, who gave a Receipt, and they prepared for toping.

After Plenty of Drinking and Talking, the Night drawing on, the happy Couple prepared for their Return Home: But as though some evil Star reigned that Day, they had no sooner began to perform the Ceremony of taking Leave, than *John* in scraping, the Floor happening to be waxed, tripped up his Heels, and he fell down on the Ground: But as People

ple that are falling, like thofe that are drowning, will catch at any Thing to fave themfelves, fo *John* catched Hold of *Joan*, and *Joan* one of the Chairs, and they all tumbled together, to the no little Mirth of the 'Squire and his Lady. But getting up, as well as they could, they began their bowing and curtfying again; and performing it now tolerably well, they left the Parlour, and entered the Court-Yard. But *Joan* reminded *John*, it would be but acting Gentlefolks like to give the Servants fomething, he turned back and gave the Footman Three-pence; and, after giving Twopence to the Coachman, who took Care of old *Dobbin*, they mounted and rode Home. It is a Matter of Difpute to this Day, between the two mannerly Couple, of which of them behaved with the greateft Gentility and Addrefs.

It fhould almoft feem needlefs, my dear *Nancy*, to make Animadverfions on this very comical Vifit; but, that you may not think I am grown indolent, I fhall juft obferve to you, that our *John* and *Joan* fhould be confidered as Examples held forth to public View, which prefent us with a ftriking Inftance of Ignorance and Vanity, Inability and Conceit.

Thofe,

Those, who aspire above the Sphere in which Providence has placed them, and soar in the Pursuit of such Things as Nature never intended for them, are making hasty Strides, if not to Ruin and Destruction, at least to Mockery and Ridicule. Had *John* and *Joan* contented themselves to behave as usual, without being over polite, their Conduct might have still remained unimpeached; but, endeavouring to effect the Manners of the 'Squire and his Lady, which are never looked for at the Plow Tail, they justly made themselves ridiculous and contemptible, and despised by even those beneath them.

I remain, &c.

T. GOODWILL

LETTER - VII.

Miss Nancy *to Master* Tommy.

Dear Tommy,

OUR Governess last Night obliged us with the Perusal of the following Meditation. I need only tell you the Author of it is your unfortunate Friend.

Conduct me, thou, of Beings, Cause divine,
Where'er I'm destin'd in thy great Design!
Freely I follow on; for should my Will
Resist, I'm impious—but must follow still!

Whoever attentively surveys the narrow Circle of human Life, will soon view, with an Eye of Indifference, the Miseries and Enjoyments that surround it. How short and momentary the former, how vain and flattering the latter, when compared with the boundless Ages of Eternity!

Happiness is the Pursuit of every Individual on this Side the silent and peaceful Grave— there all our Cares and Enjoyments cease, and there

there the Wretched and the Fortunate promiscuously mingle in their Parent Earth. The Ills of Life sit heavy on us all; we feel Disquietude a thousand Ways; we are born with Seeds of Sickness and of Sorrow, and all Infirmities spring up with Manhood. Our only Consolation is to bear with Patience, and try to smooth those Rubs we cannot possibly remove. He who enjoys an uninterrupted Series of Happiness, (if human Nature is capable of arriving at such a State) reflects with Horror and Regret on his final Dissolution; while the Miserable and Unfortunate wish for it, as the only Hopes of their Happiness. Is thy Happiness placed in the Acquisition of Wealth, beyond what is really necessary for the Enjoyment of Life?——The obtaining it shall make thee completely miserable! Dost thou seek for Happiness in the Gratification of thy youthful Passions?——Care and Infirmities shall overtake you ere you reach the Meridian of Life!

Not only the false Pleasures of the Gay and Youthful, but even the more solid and reasonable Enjoyments of domestic Happiness, frequently fall a Prey to the Malice of invidious

dious Fortune. Is thy Happiness placed in thy Partner for Life?——Fool as thou art! Sickness or Death shall deprive thee of that Blessing; or perhaps, which is worse, a Frenzy shall seize upon her Brain, which shall snatch her from thy Arms for ever. Lost to all Reason, and to every Enjoyment of Life, (it may be in the Bloom of her Youth) she shall hate and despise thee: To add to thy Misery, thou shalt see her become the Mock and Ridicule of every foolish and unthinking Brute invested with the Shape of an human Creature.

Thyrsis and *Amarante*, the Kindest Couple of Shepherd and Shepherdess that ever met, were at last unhappily parted by a most deplorable Fate. As the Mistress was one Day asleep on the Grass, a Serpent bit her on the Breast, and she died of the Wound. As soon as the Shepherd had discharged all the Funeral Rites and Duties, he erected a Monument in Honour of her Memory, and paid her daily Visits, strewing Roses and other Flowers around it, with a particular Caution, that no unclean Thing should be suffered near it.

A3

56　LETTERS *between*

As he was one Evening, either killing Worms with his Feet, or cutting them to Pieces with his Sheep hook, a Voice spoke to this Purpose: " Be not so cruel, gentle " Shepherd, to thy once-beloved *Amarante*; " for the Worms thou hast now destroyed, " with a friendly Intention, are no other than " a Part of that dear Creature; or, if I may " not be credited, lift up the Stone that " covers them, and believe thine own Eyes." He had no sooner raised the Stone, than whole Shoals came creeping out from under it, and these

these Words along with them: "Think no more what I once was; but treasure up this in thy Mind, that what *Amarante* is at present, *Thyrsis* must one Day be." This made such an Impression on the Shepherd's Mind, that he immediately quitted his Flocks, and his Herds, and devoted himself entirely to the Thoughts of Death.

A. GOODWILL

LETTER VIII.

Master Tommy *to Miss* Nancy.

Dear Nancy,

AS I find you are in the moralizing Strain, I shall trouble you with a Piece of Poetry on the Vanity of human Life. I could wish, however, that you would in your next, turn the Subject, and thereby raise my Mind from the gloomy Train of thinking, into which you have thrown it. You see that I am either elevated or depressed, just as you please. That I am not in a very merry Mood at present, the following Poem will convince you.

I.

HOW gay, at first, Life's chearful Dawn
   Attracts our pleasing Sight,
Whilst on its flow'ry Fields are drawn
   Fair Scenes of soft Delight.

II.

With Joy, alert, we swift ascend
   With trifling Baubles pleas'd;
On such our youthful Fancies bend;
   By these our Wants are eas'd.

III

Next Learning, with majeſtic Port,
   Allures us to her Side;
With Ardour we her Favour court,
   Neglecting all beſide.

IV.

Thro' ev'ry Maze we boldly ſtray,
   And ranſack all her Store;
In toilſome Studies ſpend each Day,
   Yet, panting, ſigh for more.

V.

On Manhood's Stage we next appear,
   And think to roll in joy,
But, oh! how often Woes ſevere
   Our dazzling Hopes deſtroy.

VI.

Ten thouſand Croſſes round us riſe,
   Misfortune's meagre Train,
With Gorgon* Horrors fright our Eyes,
   And fill our Souls with Pain.

---

* *Gorgon* means any Thing ugly and horrible. The Poets repreſent the *Gorgon* as a Monſter with ſnaky Hair, the Sight of which is ſaid to have turned the Beholders into Stone.

VII. Thro'

VII.

Thro' thorny Paths thus forc'd to go,
   With Grief we journey on,
Lamenting, at each pungent Throw,
   That e'er our Lives begun.

VIII.

Next hoary Age, with wrinkled Brow
   Spoils ev'ry pleasing Sense;
Our youthful Spirits cease to flow,
   And sink to Indolence.

IX.

The Gout, the Dropsy, Stone, and Rheum,
   With ev'ry tort'ring Pain,
Our Strength and Faculties consume,
   While Help's invok'd in vain.

X.

So, when Death's awful King appears,
   We ask no Power to save;
But meet his Dart, devoid of Fear,
   And court the gloomy Grave.

XI.

Then who shall ask Life's painful Boon,
   Though seeming Joys invite,
When we reflect they fade so soon,
   And Woe succeeds Delight?

XII.

Let Virtue then our Pilot be,
  Through the hard toilsome Way,
Then we'll like Autumn's Spoils remove,
  And gently glide away.

LETTER IX.

Miss Nancy *to Master* Tommy.

SO then, my dear *Tommy*, I find I have just the same Command over you, as the Weather has on the Barometer, can raise or sink the Spirits just as I please! Come then, I will disperse the Glooms of Melancholy; But let me stop here—you will say I am going to philosophise, and that you shall be obliged to put me in Mind of our Pins, Needles, and Thread papers.

The Poem, you last favoured us with, has afforded us great Satisfaction, and has already passed three Readings and gained the royal Assent from our Governess, who, to oblige us, and turn the Subject, gave us the following Tale.

Not many hundred Years ago, there was a Queen so very old, that she had neither Teeth nor Hair; her Head shook like an Aspen Leaf, that trembles at every Breath of Wind. She could not see even through her Spectacles,
and

and her Nose and Chin met close together. She was grown shorter by one Half than what she once had been, and all of a Heap, with her Back so round, that one would have imagined she had been crooked all her Lifetime.

A Fairy, who had been present at her Birth, approached her, and asked her if she was desirous of growing young again. The Queen replied, in the greatest Extacy, she would give all the rich Jewels she had, to be but twenty years old. We must then, (said the Fairy) find out some person who will assume your Age, whose Bloom and Health must be transferred to you. On whom shall we bestow your hundred Years?

The Queen ordered strict Search to be made throughout her Kingdom, to find out one, who would accept of the Infirmities of Age to make her young again. Several Vagrants offered their Service, who, to become rich, would submit to be old; but, when they saw what a Figure the old Queen was, how she rattled in her Throat, lived upon Spoon-Meat, how dirty she was, and,

in

in short, such a figure as Decency will not permit a particular Description of, they declined her Load of Years, and chose rather to beg their Bread, and be cloathed in Rags.

After this there came several ambitious Persons, to whom she made large Promises of future Honours and Employments. But of what Service, (said they, as soon as they saw her) would such Honours be to us? We should be ashamed to shew our Heads, should we become so hideous and loathsome. At length there appeared a young Country Lass, fair as the Day, who proposed to accept of the Crown in Exchange for her Youth. Her Name was *Peronella*.

At first the Queen was very angry; but to what Purpose?—She was resolved to be young again. Let us divide the Kingdom, said she: You shall have one Half, and I the other: This is a Reward surely sufficient for you, who are but a poor Country Lass. No, replied *Peronella*, it is not sufficient for me. I will have it all. Let me still be a poor Country Girl as I am, with my fresh Complexion, and do you keep your hundred Years with all your Wrinkles, and Death himself, who treads upon your Heels.

But then, replied the Queen, what shall I do, if I resign my Kingdom? You will laugh, dance and sing, as I do, replied *Peronella*, and, having thus said, she laughed, danced and sung before her. The Queen who could do nothing like it, expressed her Doubts, that *Peronella*, who was a stranger to the Infirmities of Age, would be sadly at a Loss to know how to behave herself in her Place. Though the silly Country Girl would not pretend to answer for her Behaviour, yet, as she apprehended there was something very great in being a Queen, she was mighty desirous of making the Experiment.

While

While they were thus arguing the Point, the Fairy came in, who asked the Country Girl, if she was willing to serve the Apprenticeship of an old Queen, and try whether she liked the Trade. The Girl answered in the Affirmative. In a Moment Wrinkles cover all her Forehead, her Hair turns Grey, she becomes peevish and ill-natured, her Head shakes, her Teeth drop out, and she is already an hundred Years old. The Fairy opens a little Box, and out starts a numerous Throng of Officer and Courtiers richly dress, who grew to their full Stature as fast as they came out, and paid a thousand Compliments to the new Queen. A splendid Entertainment is prepared for her; but she has no Appetite, and cannot chew; she is ashamed and confounded, knowing not what to say, or how to behave; she coughs till she is just expiring, and drivels on her Chin; a Drop hangs at her Nose, which she wipes off with her Sleeve; she peers in her Looking glass, and observes, that she was grown more wrinkled and deformed than an old Grandam Ape.

In the mean Time the real Queen stood in a Corner, smiled and began to grow plump and

and jolly; her Hair grew again, and she bred new teeth; her Complexion became fresh and sanguine, she straitened, and had a thousand pretty Ways, but was nasty; her Petticoats were short, and her Gown seemed as dusty as if she had sifted Cinders in it. She was never accustomed to such a Garb, and the Guards, taking her for some common Scullion, would have drove her headlong out of the Palace.

Then *Peronella* said to her, I perceive it is a Torment to you not to be a Queen, and a greater to me to be one: Here, take your Crown again, and give me my grey Petticoat. The Exchange was instantly made, the Queen grew old again, and *Peronella* young. Before the Transformation was well finished, they both repented; but then it was too late. The Fairy doomed them for ever to remain in their own Station. The Queen wept every Day, if her Finger did but ake. She would cry, Alas! was I now *Peronella*, I should lodge in a poor Cottage, and live indeed on Chesnuts; but then I should dance with the Shepherds, under the Shady Elm, to the soft Music of the Flute.

Flute. Of what Service is a Bed of Down to me, since I am restless and uneasy? or a numerous Retinne, since they cannot ease my Pain? Her Impatience was an Addition to her Disorder; and her twelve Physicians, who were constantly in waiting, still encreased it. At length, in about two Month's Time, she died.

Peronella was dancing with her Companions upon the verdant Banks of a purling Stream, when she first heard of the Queens's Death. Then she was conscious that she was more fortunate in the Loss, than prudent in the Choice of a Kingdom.

Let me remind you, my little Pupils, continued our Governess, that this Tale is the Production of Fancy only; I have, indeed, long since taught you totally to disregard the Doctrine of Giants, Fairies, and such like idle Inventions. This Tale, however, affords an excellent Lesson of Morality: It explores the Vanity and Restlessness of the human Heart, which is ever aspiring to such Things, as, when obtained, frequently prove pernicious, often fatal. I will for once treat you like

Women

nd remind you of that Age, in
have cried over a Play-thing, after
led it to Pieces to view its Con-
en now, how eager are you in the
ʾruits, which pall the Appetite, and
prove pernicious to the Health?
w up in Years, so will a restless
 increase with you, unless nipp'd
 Though the Love of Novelty, or
on of being great, rich, or power-
duce you to envy the Condition of
 thinking how happy you should
ɔu but in their Place, yet remem-
 only the external Part; the deep
 the Mind are hidden from your
u see the State and Grandeur that
ttend Royalty, and those in ex-
ns, but you see not the Servility
Meanness which such People are
educed to. Whatever then may
ure Lot, be contented, and rest
ured, that there is no one Person
World, however exalted in Sta-
ıe, or Honours, that you would
 possible, to personate. Like Pe-
ı would soon return to yourself
ıat something, which, amidst Po-
verty

verty and Contempt, amidſt Age and Infirmities, every one poſſeſſes. Thus ſays Mr. *Pope*:

Whate'er the Paſſion, Knowledge, Fame or Pelf,
Not one will change his Neighbour with himſelf.
The Learn'd is happy Nature to explore,
The Fool is happy that he knows no more;
The Rich is happy in the Plenty given,
The Poor contents him with the Care of Heav'n.
See the blind Beggar dance, the Cripple ſing,
The Sot a Hero, Lunatic a King;
The ſtarving Chemiſt in his golden Views
Supremely bleſt, the Poet in his Muſe.
See ſome ſtrange Comfort ev'ry State attend,
And Pride beſtow'd on all a common Friend.

I remain, &c.

A. GOODWILL.

LETTER X.

Master Tommy *to Miss* Nancy.

My dear Nancy,

BEING Yesterday Afternoon very sleepy, I took a comfortable Nap in the Arbour, when I dreamt many odd and unaccountable Things. I thought myself got into a strange House, in the Parlour of which was a Lady sitting and teaching her good Children to read; and in another Part a Lady beating her Servant most cruelly, as you here see represented.

72 LETTERS *between*

The next Moment I thought myself in a Palace, in which the King stood with a Sword in his Hand, and a Number of Ladies seated in a Cluster on the Floor, as you here see:

But what was the Meaning of all this I could not understand, and, as I then thought, I dared not to enquire. In another Apartment of this Palace I beheld the following Picture, which much attracted my Attention.

Master Tommy and Miss Nancy. 73

You here see a poor unhappy Man ready to fall a Victim to Death, whose Dart is lifted up on high to strike him; but the Eye of Providence and Mercy interferes and prevents it. It is this Eye of Providence, my dear Nancy, that protects us in our Journey through Life, and secures us from Dangers that hourly await us. While I was making Reflections like this, I suddenly awoke, and determined to acquaint you with the Substance of my Dream, and herewith send you the Drawings I made from these imaginary Objects.

I remain, &c.
T. GOODWILL.

LETTER XI.

Miss Nancy *to Master* Tommy.

Dear Tommy,

I Will not make any Comments on your wonderful Dream. I am obliged to you for it, as well as for the excellent Drawings which accompanied it. In return, I will trouble you with the following Story as related to us by our Governess.

Some Time ago there came to settle in this City a Lady of Family and Fortune. She was visited by us all; but she had so deep a Melancholy, arising, as it appeared, from an ill State of Health, that no friendly Hand could afford her the least Relief, or induce her to be chearful. In this Condition she languished among us for five Years, still continuing every Day to grow worse.

Her

Master Tommy and Miss Nancy. 75

Her Fate was lamented by us all: Her Flesh was withered away: her Appetite decayed by Degrees, till all Food became nauseous to her Sight; her Strength failed her; her Feet could not support her tottering Body, lean and worn away as it was, and we expected every Hour would be her last. One Day she called her most intimate Friends to her Bed-side, and, as well as she could, spoke to them to the following Purpose: "I know

"you all pity me. But, alas! I am not so
"much the Object of your Pity as your Con-
"tempt; for all my Misery is of my own
"seeking

"seeking, and owning to the Wickedness of
"my own Mind. I had two Sisters, with
"whom I was bred up; and I have all my
"Life-time been unhappy, for no other Cause
"but their Success in the World. When we
"were young, I could neither eat nor sleep in
"Peace when they had either Praise or Plea-
"sure. When we grew up to be Women
"they were both soon married much to their
"Advantage and Satisfaction. This galled
"me to the Heart; and, though I had several
"good Offers, yet, as I did not think them
"in all Respects equal to my Sisters, I would
"not accept them, and yet was inwardly vexed
"to refuse them, for Fear I should get no
"better. I generally deliberated so long,
"that I lost my Lovers, and then I pined for
"that Loss. I never wanted for any Thing,
"and was in a Situation, in which I might
"have been happy, if I would. My Sister,
"loved me very well, for I concealed from
"them as much as possible my odious Envy;
"and yet never did any unhappy Mortal
"lead so wretched a Life as I have; for every
"Blessing they enjoyed was a Dagger to my
"Heart. It is this Envy that has caused my
"ill State of Health, has preyed upon my

"very

"very Vitals, and will now bring me to my
"Grave." The very next Day she died.

Let me remind you, my little Pupils, that Envy is the most unnatural and unaccountable of all the Passions. There is scarce any other Emotion of the Mind, however unreasonable, but may have something said in Excuse for it, and there are many of these Weaknesses of the Soul, which notwithstanding the Wrongfulness and Irregularity of them swell the Heart, while they last, with Pleasure and Gladness: But the envious Person has no such Apology as this to make. The stronger the Passion is, the greater Torment they endure, and subject themselves to a continued real Pain by only wishing Ill to others. Revenge is sweet, though cruel and inhuman, and though it sometimes thirsts even for Blood, yet may be glutted and satiated. Avarice is something highly monstrous and absurd, yet as it is a Desire after Riches, every little Acquisition gives it Pleasure, and to behold and feel the hoarded Treasure, to a covetous Person, is a constant uncloying Enjoyment. But Envy, which is an Anxiety arising in our Minds upon our observing Accomplishments in others, which we want ourselves, can never receive any true Comfort, unless in a Deluge, a Conflagration, a Plague, or some general Calamity that should befal the human being; for as long as there is a creature living, that enjoys its Existence happily within the envious Person's Sphere, it will afford Nourishment to its distempered Mind, but such Nourishment as will make them pine and fret, and emaciate themselves to nothing. It is not in the Power of the most cruel Tyrant to invent a Torture more painful and severe, than that with which envious People punish themselves.

LETTER

LETTER XII.

Master Tommy *to Miss* Nancy

Dear Sister,

AS I find the Time is now nearly approaching, when our Correspondence must be put an End to, and we return to such Studies as our Superiors shall please to direct, in Order to caution you against the fatal Effects of Luxury and Indolence, I shall present your little Companions with the following instructive Story.

Hacho, a King of *Lapland,* was in his Youth the most renowned of the Northern Warriors. His martial Atchievements remain engraven on a Pillar of Flint in the Rocks of *Hanga,* and are to this Day solemnly carolled to the Harp by the *Laplanders,* at the Fires, with which they celebrate their nightly Festivals.

Such

Such was his intrepid Spirit, that he ventured to pass the Lake *Vether* to the Isles of *Wizards*, where he descended alone into the dreary Vault, in which a Magician had been kept bound for six Ages, and read the *Gothic* Characters inscribed on his brazen Mace. His Eyes were so piercing that, as ancient Chronicles report, he could blunt his Weapons only by looking at them. At twelve Years of Age he carried an Iron Vessel of a prodigious Weight, for the Length of five Furlongs, in Presence of all the Chiefs of his Father's Castle.

His Prudence and Wisdom were equally celebrated. Two of his Proverbs are yet remembered and repeated among the *Laplanders*. To express the Vigilance of the Supreme Being, he was won't to say, Odin's *Belt is always buckled*. To shew that the most prosperous Condition of Life is often hazardous, his Lesson was, *When you slide on the smooth Ice, beware of Pits beneath*. He consoled his Countrymen, when they were once preparing to leave the frozen Deserts of *Lapland*, and resolved to seek some warmer Climate, by telling them, that the Eastern Nations, notwithstanding their boasted Fertillity, passed every Night

Night amidst the Horrors of anxious Apprehension, and were inexpressively affrighted, and almost stunned, every Morning with the Noise of the Sun while he was rising.

His Temperance and Severity of Manners were his chief Praise. In his early Years he never tasted Wine, nor would he drink out of a painted Cup. He constantly slept in his Armour, with his Spear in his Hand, nor would he use a Battle-Axe whose Handle was inlaid with Brass. He did not, however, persevere in his Contempt of Luxury, nor did he close his Days with Honour.

One Evening, after hunting the Gulos, or wild Dog, being bewildered in a solitary Forest, and having passed the Fatigues of the Day without any Interval of Refreshment, he discovered a large Store of Honey in the Hollow of a Pine. This was a Dainty which he had never tasted before, and being at once faint and hungry, he fell greedily upon it. From this unusual and delicious Repast he received so much Satisfaction, that, at his Return Home, he commanded Honey to be served up at his Table every Day.

His

His Palate, by Degrees, became refined and vitiated; he began to lose his native Relish for simple Fare, and contracted a Habit of indulging himself in Delicacies: He ordered the delightful Gardens of his Castle to be thrown open, in which the richest Fruits had been suffered to ripen and decay, unobserved and untouched, for many revolving Autumns, and gratified his Appetite with luxurious Deserts.

At length he found it expedient to introduce Wine, as an agreeable Improvement, or a necessary Ingredient, to his new Way of Living; and having once tasted it, he was tempted, by little and little, to give a Loose to the Excesses of Intoxication. His general Simplicity of Life was changed; he perfumed his Apartments, by burning the Wood of the most aromatic Fir, and commanded his Helmet to be ornamented with beautiful Rows of the Teeth of the Rein Deer. Indolence and Effeminacy stole upon him by pleasing and imperceptible Gradations, which relaxed the Sinews of his Resolution, and extinguished his Thirst of military Glory.

While *Hacho* was thus immersed in Pleasure and Repose, it was reported to him, one Morning, that the preceding Night a disastrous Omen had been discovered, and that Bats and hedious Birds had drank up the Oil which nourished the perpetual Lamp in the Temple of *Odin*. About the same Time, a Messenger arrived to tell him, that the King of *Norway* had invaded his Kingdom with a formidable Army.

Hacho, terrified as he was with the Omen of the Night, and enervated with Indolence, roused himself from his voluptuous Lethargy, and recollecting some faint and few Sparks of veteran Valour, marched forward to meet him. Both Armies joined Battle in the Forest where *Hacho* had been lost after Hunting; and it so happened, that the King of *Norway* challenged him to single Combat near the Place where he had tasted the Honey. The *Lapland* Chief, languid and long disused to Arms, was soon overpowered; he fell to the Ground, and before his insulting Adversary struck his Head from his Body, he uttered this Exclamation, which the *Laplanders* still use as an early Lesson to their Children; " The vi-
" cious

" cious Man should date his Destruction from
" the first Temptation. How justly do I fall
" a Sacrifice to Sloth and Luxury, in the
" Place where I first yielded to those Allure-
" ments, which induced me to deviate from
" Temperance and Innocence: The Honey
" which I tasted in this Forest, and not the
" Hand of the King of *Norway*, conquers
" *Hacho*."

I cannot help thinking I now see a tender Tear falling from the Eye of my Compassionate *Nancy*, as the only Tribute she can pay to the Memory of the unfortunate *Hacho*. What is here

here said of this famous *Laplander*, may be applicable enough to many in lower Conditions of Life, who begin the World with a virtuous Intrepdity, seemingly to be conquered by neither Difficulties nor Dangers; but, by some fatal Accident, are tempted to taste the Honey of Folly, which immediately vitiates the Palate, and corrupts the whole Frame. It is Madness to prescribe Bounds to Virtue; for they who once quit that thorny Path, and stray through the blooming and enchanting Grove of Pleasure, will hardly be persuaded to return, but go on, till, like the wretched *Hacho*, they meet with Ruin and Destruction.

LET-

LETTER XIII.

Miss Nancy *to Master* Tommy.

Dear Tommy,

OUR little Assembly is at this Moment in full Convocation in the Arbour, from whence I now write to you. Your *Hacho* has made a very sensible Impression on our Minds, and we should have been very g'ad to convince you, how much we are improved in moral Reflections: But we have just received Orders to attend School To-morrow. I am, however, particularly desired to send you the Thanks of the whole Assembly, who desire you to accept of a Pair of worked Ruffles, as a small Testimony of our Gratitude, hoping, at a future convenient Season, you will oblige us again in the same Manner.

Your most affectionate Sister,

A. GOODWILL.

LETTER XIV.

Master Tommy *to Miss* Nancy.

My dearest Nancy,

I THANK you and your Assembly for the kind Present you have sent me, which I shall carefully preserve as a Premium from the Society of Arts. You, my pretty *Nancy*, had the first Word, I must have the last.

Your apparent Regret, that you want Time to say more, brings to my Mind a Saying of *Seneca:* " We all of us complain of
" the Shortness of Time, and almost all of
" us have much more than we know what to
" do with. Our Lives are spent either in
" doing nothing at all, or in doing nothing
" to the Purpose, or in doing nothing that
" we ought to do: We are always complain-
" ing our Days are few, and at the same
" Time acting as though there would be no
" End of them."

Though we seem grieved at the Shortness of Life in general, we are wishing every Period

riod of it at an End. The Minor longs to be at Age, then to be a Man of Business, then to make up an Estate, then to arrive at Honours, then to retire. Thus, though the whole Life is allowed by every one to be very short, the several Divisions of it appear long and tedious. We are for lengthening our Span in general, but would fain contract the Parts of which it is composed. The Usurer would be very well satisfied to have all the Time annihilated, that lies between the present Moment and the next Quarter Day. The Politician would be contented to loose three Years of his Life, could he place Things in the Posture, which he fancies they will stand in after such a Revolution of Time. Thus, as fast as our Time runs, we should be very glad, in most Parts of our Lives, that it ran much faster than it does. Several Hours of the Day hang upon our Hands, nay, we often wish away whole Years, and travel through Time as through a Country filled with many wild and empty Wastes, which we would fain hurry over, that we may arrive at those several little Settlements, or imaginary Points of Rest, which are dispersed up and down in it. We must not, like the silly Boy in the Picture

I here

Master TOMMY *and Miss* NANCY.   89

I here send you, run after Time: We must keep the Lead of him.

If we divide the Life of most People into twenty Parts, we shall find, that at least nineteen of them are meer Gaps and Chasms, which are neither filled with Pleasure nor Business. I do not, however, include in this Calculation the Life of those, who are in a perpetual Hurry of Affairs, but of those only, who are not always engaged in Scenes of Action. I will tell you, my dear *Nancy*, how I would have you little People fill up your Time.

The

The first is the Exercise of Virtue in th[e] most general Acceptation of the Word. T[o] advise the Ignorant, relieve the Needy, com[-] fort the Afflicted, are Duties that fall in ou[r] Way almost every Day of our Lives.

The next Method that I would propose t[o] fill up your Time, should be useful and inn[o-] cent Diversions. I must confess, I think it b[e-] low reasonable Creatures to be altogether c[on-] versant in such Diversions as are merely inn[o-] cent, and that have nothing else to recom[-] mend them, but that there is no Hurt [in] them. Whether any Kind of Gaming h[as] even thus much to say for itself, I shall not de[-] termine; but I think it is very wonderful, t[o] see little Folks passing away Hours togethe[r] in shuffling and dividing a Pack of Card[s] with no other Conversation, than that wh[ich] is made up of a few Game Phrases, and [no] other Ideas, but those of red or black Spo[ts] ranged together in different Figures. Wou[ld] not a Person laugh to hear such a one com[-] plaining that Life is short!

The Mind never unbends itself so agree[a-] bly, as in the Conversation of a well-chose[n] Frien[d]

www.ingramcontent.com/pod-product-compliance
Lightning Source LLC
Chambersburg PA
CBHW032245080426
42735CB00008B/1007